PRINCEWILL LAGANG

Courtship in Christ: A Path to Godly Marriage

First published by PRINCEWILL LAGANG 2023

Copyright © 2023 by Princewill Lagang

All rights reserved. No part of this publication may be reproduced, stored or transmitted in any form or by any means, electronic, mechanical, photocopying, recording, scanning, or otherwise without written permission from the publisher. It is illegal to copy this book, post it to a website, or distribute it by any other means without permission.

Princewill Lagang asserts the moral right to be identified as the author of this work.

First edition

This book was professionally typeset on Reedsy.
Find out more at reedsy.com

Contents

1	Courtship in Christ: A Path to Godly Marriage	1
2	The Biblical Foundation of Courtship in Christ	4
3	Navigating the Early Stages of Courtship in Christ	7
4	Deepening the Connection: Courtship and Engagement	10
5	The Godly Union: Christian Marriage and Beyond	13
6	Navigating Life Together: Communication, Challenges, and...	16
7	Growing Together in Faith and Love	19
8	An Enduring Legacy: Reflecting on Courtship in Christ	22
9	Resources and Additional Guidance	25
10	A Lifelong Journey of Love, Faith, and Commitment	28
11	Embracing Godly Marriage in a Changing World	31
12	A Lifelong Covenant of Love and Faith	34

1

Courtship in Christ: A Path to Godly Marriage

In a world marked by rapid social and technological changes, the concept of courtship has evolved considerably. Traditional dating practices have given way to modern approaches, but the timeless desire for love, companionship, and lasting commitment remains unaltered. It is within the context of these shifting societal landscapes that we embark on a journey exploring "Courtship in Christ: A Path to Godly Marriage."

1.1 Introduction

The pursuit of a godly marriage has been a central aspect of human existence throughout history. From biblical tales of Adam and Eve to the modern-day aspirations of countless individuals, the quest for a meaningful, fulfilling marriage transcends cultural and temporal boundaries. This chapter delves into the heart of courtship in the context of Christian faith, laying the foundation for a profound exploration of this timeless institution.

1.2 The Contemporary Dilemma

The contemporary approach to romantic relationships is a far cry from the biblical concept of courtship. The rapid expansion of online dating, social media, and a culture of instant gratification has significantly altered the way we meet, connect, and form relationships. The consequences are evident: higher divorce rates, a pervasive sense of emptiness in relationships, and a general sense of disillusionment regarding the institution of marriage.

1.3 The Role of Faith

Amidst these changes, people of faith seek a path that reflects their beliefs, values, and convictions. The Christian perspective on courtship is grounded in faith and spirituality. It values commitment, selflessness, and the belief that a marriage should be a reflection of one's devotion to God. Courtship in Christ is not merely about finding a life partner but also about growing closer to God in the process.

1.4 The Purpose of This Book

This book is designed to serve as a guide, an inspiration, and a resource for individuals who wish to embark on a journey of courtship in Christ. It draws upon biblical wisdom, Christian principles, and contemporary insights to offer a comprehensive understanding of the concept. We will explore the various stages of courtship, from the initial meeting to engagement and, ultimately, marriage. It will address important topics such as discernment, communication, and the role of the church community.

1.5 What to Expect

Throughout this book, we will engage with real-life stories of couples who have successfully walked the path of courtship in Christ, as well as those who have faced challenges and overcome them with faith. We will discuss practical advice, scriptural guidance, and the importance of prayer and discernment. Each chapter will be a stepping stone on the path to understanding, fostering, and sustaining a godly marriage.

1.6 Conclusion

The first chapter serves as a foundation for the journey we are about to undertake. It establishes the context for exploring courtship in Christ, the challenges posed by modern dating, and the role of faith in finding and nurturing a godly marriage. As we continue, we will dive deeper into the intricacies of this sacred journey, bringing together the wisdom of the ages with the vitality of the present to guide us toward a life enriched by love, faith, and commitment.

2

The Biblical Foundation of Courtship in Christ

2.1 Introduction

To embark on the journey of courtship in Christ, it is essential to establish a solid foundation rooted in the rich biblical teachings that guide our faith and relationships. In this chapter, we will explore the fundamental principles of courtship as outlined in the Bible, seeking wisdom, guidance, and inspiration from scripture.

2.2 God's Design for Marriage

The Bible begins with the divine creation of Adam and Eve, the first man and woman. This foundational story in Genesis underscores God's intention for marriage—a union designed to be a lifelong partnership, characterized by love, mutual support, and the pursuit of His divine purpose. It is in the context of this divine design that courtship in Christ takes shape.

2.3 Love, Selflessness, and Sacrifice

The Bible teaches us about love in its purest form. In 1 Corinthians 13, we find a description of love that is patient, kind, not envious, not self-seeking, and always protecting and persevering. This scriptural definition serves as a guiding light for Christian courtship. It emphasizes selflessness, sacrifice, and the mutual uplifting of one's partner in the pursuit of a godly marriage.

2.4 Seeking God's Will

Proverbs 3:6 encourages us to "acknowledge God in all our ways, and He will direct our paths." This principle is essential in Christian courtship. Seeking God's will through prayer, discernment, and consultation with wise spiritual advisors is a pivotal aspect of the journey toward a godly marriage.

2.5 Courting with Purpose

Courtship in Christ is purpose-driven. It involves more than simply dating for the sake of companionship or pleasure. It is a commitment to pursuing a partner who shares your faith and values, and together, working towards a shared purpose in God's plan.

2.6 The Role of Parents and Community

The Bible acknowledges the significance of community in the process of courtship. Parents, spiritual mentors, and the church community play vital roles in guiding, supporting, and affirming the relationship. Their wisdom and discernment can provide valuable insight during the courtship journey.

2.7 Chastity and Purity

The Bible also underscores the importance of chastity and purity in courtship. Maintaining physical and emotional purity is an expression of reverence for the sacred nature of marriage. Scriptures like 1 Thessalonians 4:3-5 encourage believers to "abstain from sexual immorality" and to "learn to control your body in a way that is holy and honorable."

2.8 Conclusion

This chapter has laid the biblical foundation for courtship in Christ. It has explored the divine design of marriage, the principles of love, selflessness, and sacrifice, the importance of seeking God's will, courting with purpose, the role of parents and community, and the value of chastity and purity. These principles will serve as our guiding stars as we progress through the stages of courtship in Christ, seeking to fulfill our calling to a godly marriage that glorifies God. In the following chapters, we will delve deeper into practical aspects of courtship and address common challenges and questions that arise along the way.

3

Navigating the Early Stages of Courtship in Christ

3.1 Introduction

As we continue our exploration of "Courtship in Christ: A Path to Godly Marriage," this chapter delves into the early stages of courtship. These are the moments when two individuals first connect, showing interest in one another and beginning to build the foundation of a Christian relationship.

3.2 The Initial Connection

The journey of courtship often begins with a simple yet profound connection. It may be through church activities, mutual friends, or a shared faith-based group. This initial meeting lays the groundwork for further exploration.

3.3 Getting to Know Each Other

In Christian courtship, the process of getting to know each other is deliberate and thoughtful. It involves deep conversations about faith, values, goals, and dreams. This stage is marked by patience and a genuine desire to understand the other person on a spiritual and emotional level.

3.4 Prayer and Discernment

One of the distinguishing features of courtship in Christ is the role of prayer and discernment. Couples seek God's guidance and direction in their relationship. Proverbs 3:5-6 reminds us to "trust in the Lord with all your heart and lean not on your understanding; in all your ways submit to him, and he will make your paths straight." Prayer is the cornerstone of decision-making in courtship.

3.5 Setting Boundaries

Boundaries are an essential component of Christian courtship. They help maintain chastity and purity, ensuring that the focus remains on building a spiritual connection. Setting and respecting physical, emotional, and spiritual boundaries is a sign of respect for oneself and one's partner.

3.6 The Role of Accountability

Christian courtship often involves accountability to parents, mentors, or trusted friends. These individuals provide valuable guidance and support, ensuring that the courtship stays on a godly path and that both individuals are making wise choices.

3.7 Communication

Effective communication is key in any relationship, and it is no different in courtship. Learning to communicate openly, honestly, and respectfully with your partner is crucial for building a strong foundation.

3.8 Challenges and Questions

This chapter will address common challenges and questions that arise during the early stages of courtship. These might include issues related to family approval, differing values, and the need for patience.

3.9 Conclusion

The early stages of courtship in Christ are marked by a deep and purposeful connection, guided by prayer, discernment, and boundaries. Effective communication and the involvement of trusted advisors play significant roles. In the chapters to come, we will continue our journey through courtship in Christ, exploring the transition from courtship to engagement and ultimately to the fulfillment of a godly marriage.

4

Deepening the Connection: Courtship and Engagement

4.1 Introduction

In the journey of "Courtship in Christ: A Path to Godly Marriage," we now move from the early stages of courtship into the period of deepening connection and engagement. This chapter explores the pivotal transition where the courtship matures into a more committed and serious relationship.

4.2 Strengthening the Spiritual Bond

As the courtship deepens, so does the spiritual bond between the couple. This is the time for shared prayer, devotionals, and the exploration of how faith will be at the center of the marital relationship. The couple is encouraged to attend church together, participate in Bible studies, and seek spiritual growth as a united front.

4.3 Preparing for a Godly Marriage

The courtship journey in Christ is not just about finding a partner but also about preparing for a godly marriage. Couples are encouraged to seek premarital counseling and guidance from wise, experienced mentors to ensure they are well-prepared for the challenges and joys that marriage brings.

4.4 Ring of Commitment

The exchange of engagement rings symbolizes a significant milestone in courtship. These rings serve as a tangible reminder of the commitment to marry and the vows made to one another and to God.

4.5 Challenges and Preparations

This chapter will also address the challenges and preparations that come with the engagement phase. These challenges may include wedding planning, family dynamics, and financial considerations. It is important for the couple to rely on their faith and the guidance of mentors during this time.

4.6 The Role of Family and Community

Families and the church community continue to play an essential role in guiding and supporting the couple during engagement. Their wisdom, encouragement, and prayers are invaluable as the couple moves closer to a godly marriage.

4.7 Maintaining Purity and Chastity

The call to maintain purity and chastity does not diminish during engagement; in fact, it becomes even more critical. The engaged couple must continue to honor God's plan for sexual purity and remain committed to their spiritual journey.

4.8 Preparing for the Wedding

While the focus is on preparing for a godly marriage, the practical aspects of wedding planning are also significant. This chapter will discuss how to balance the spiritual and practical preparations, ensuring the wedding reflects the couple's faith and values.

4.9 Conclusion

The transition from courtship to engagement is a significant step in the journey of courtship in Christ. It marks a deepening of the spiritual connection and a commitment to marriage. Throughout this phase, maintaining purity and seeking guidance from family and the church community remain paramount. As we continue our exploration in the following chapters, we will address the final steps towards a godly marriage, including the wedding ceremony and the lifelong commitment it represents.

5

The Godly Union: Christian Marriage and Beyond

5.1 Introduction

In this chapter of "Courtship in Christ: A Path to Godly Marriage," we arrive at the culmination of the courtship journey – the wedding ceremony, the sacrament of Christian marriage, and the lifelong commitment that follows.

5.2 The Sanctity of Christian Marriage

Christian marriage is viewed as a sacred union ordained by God. The Bible, in Ephesians 5:31, states that "a man will leave his father and mother and be united to his wife, and the two will become one flesh." This profound union signifies a spiritual and emotional oneness, a bond reflective of Christ's love for the Church.

5.3 The Wedding Ceremony

The wedding ceremony is the public declaration and celebration of this holy union. It is a time for the couple to make their vows before God, their families, and their community. The ceremony is typically held in a church and is filled with scriptural readings, prayers, and songs that reflect the couple's faith and commitment.

5.4 Marriage Vows

The vows exchanged during the wedding ceremony are a pivotal moment. They serve as promises made not only to one's spouse but to God. These vows often include pledges of love, fidelity, and a commitment to support and cherish one another.

5.5 The Role of the Church Community

The church community plays an essential role in supporting and nurturing the newlywed couple. This support extends beyond the wedding day, as the church becomes a source of guidance, encouragement, and accountability for the marriage.

5.6 The First Year of Marriage

The first year of marriage can be challenging as the couple adjusts to their new life together. This chapter offers insights into overcoming common challenges and building a strong foundation for a lifelong, godly marriage.

5.7 Maintaining a Strong Spiritual Connection

A godly marriage requires an ongoing spiritual connection. Couples are encouraged to pray together, engage in regular Bible study, and seek God's guidance for their marriage. This spiritual foundation serves as a source of strength and unity throughout their journey.

5.8 Challenges and Renewal

Over the years, every marriage faces challenges. This chapter will also address common issues that couples may encounter and provide guidance on how to renew their commitment and keep their marriage grounded in Christ.

5.9 Conclusion

This chapter concludes the journey from courtship to Christian marriage. The wedding ceremony represents the culmination of the courtship in Christ, and the marriage vows serve as a lifelong commitment to God and one another. As the couple enters into marriage, they do so with a profound sense of faith, love, and unity, and with the support and guidance of their church community. In the upcoming chapters, we will explore the ongoing aspects of marriage, including communication, raising a family, and growing together in faith and love.

6

Navigating Life Together: Communication, Challenges, and Family

6.1 Introduction

In the continuing journey of "Courtship in Christ: A Path to Godly Marriage," this chapter explores the intricacies of navigating life as a married couple. It delves into the importance of effective communication, addressing common challenges, and the significant role that family plays in the context of Christian marriage.

6.2 Effective Communication

Communication is the cornerstone of a successful marriage. This section emphasizes the importance of open, honest, and respectful communication between spouses. It explores active listening, conflict resolution, and maintaining a strong emotional connection.

6.3 Spiritual Growth as a Couple

A godly marriage involves continuous spiritual growth as a couple. The chapter discusses the importance of attending church together, reading the Bible as a team, and participating in faith-based activities that strengthen the spiritual bond between spouses.

6.4 Facing Challenges

Challenges are an inevitable part of married life. This chapter addresses common challenges such as financial struggles, career stress, and changes in family dynamics. It provides guidance on how to approach these difficulties while remaining rooted in faith.

6.5 Raising a Family

For many couples, raising a family is a central aspect of their journey. This section discusses the Christian perspective on parenting, emphasizing the importance of instilling faith and values in children, creating a loving and supportive home environment, and seeking guidance from Scripture.

6.6 The Role of Extended Family

Family remains a significant influence in the lives of married couples. It is essential to maintain healthy boundaries while nurturing relationships with extended family members. The chapter offers insights on striking a balance and fostering positive connections.

6.7 Celebrating Milestones

Milestones, whether they be anniversaries, achievements, or spiritual awakenings, are moments to celebrate and reflect on the journey as a couple. This section explores the significance of marking these occasions with gratitude and joy.

6.8 Conclusion

Navigating life together as a married couple in the context of "Courtship in Christ" is a multifaceted endeavor. Effective communication, spiritual growth, addressing challenges, and nurturing family relationships are essential aspects of this journey. As we progress through the final chapters of this book, we will explore the lifelong commitment that a godly marriage represents, offer guidance on growing together in faith, and provide insights into maintaining a strong, Christ-centered relationship.

7

Growing Together in Faith and Love

7.1 Introduction

As we approach the concluding chapters of "Courtship in Christ: A Path to Godly Marriage," this chapter explores the lifelong journey of growing together in faith and love. A godly marriage is not just a one-time commitment but an ongoing endeavor to deepen one's relationship with God and one's spouse.

7.2 Continual Spiritual Growth

A vital aspect of a godly marriage is the continued spiritual growth of both spouses. This section discusses the importance of setting aside time for prayer, Bible study, and spiritual reflection as a couple. It also encourages exploring faith-based activities together to strengthen the spiritual bond.

7.3 Acts of Service and Love

In a Christian marriage, love is not merely a feeling but an action. This chapter delves into the significance of selfless acts of service and love, following the example of Christ's love for the Church. Acts of kindness, forgiveness, and support are key in maintaining a strong bond.

7.4 Overcoming Trials and Challenges

Every marriage faces trials and challenges. These can come in various forms, such as health issues, financial difficulties, or personal conflicts. This section offers guidance on approaching these challenges with faith, resilience, and mutual support.

7.5 Relationship Enrichment

To continue growing in love and faith, couples are encouraged to seek relationship enrichment. This may include attending marriage retreats, participating in counseling, or reading marriage-enhancing books. These efforts help couples invest in their relationship and keep it strong.

7.6 Fostering Friendship and Companionship

Friendship is a foundational element of a godly marriage. This chapter emphasizes the importance of maintaining a deep and abiding friendship with one's spouse. Spending quality time together, pursuing common interests, and sharing life's joys and sorrows all contribute to a strong marital friendship.

7.7 The Legacy of a Godly Marriage

A godly marriage leaves a lasting legacy, both for the couple's own lives and for future generations. This section discusses the impact of a Christ-centered marriage on children, the community, and society at large.

7.8 Conclusion

Growing together in faith and love is a lifelong journey for couples committed to "Courtship in Christ." This chapter explores the ongoing aspects of maintaining a strong spiritual bond, facing challenges with faith, and investing in the love and companionship that a godly marriage offers. As we approach the concluding chapter, we will reflect on the profound journey of "Courtship in Christ" and the enduring legacy it leaves.

8

An Enduring Legacy: Reflecting on Courtship in Christ

8.1 Introduction

In the final chapter of "Courtship in Christ: A Path to Godly Marriage," we reflect on the profound journey of courtship in Christ, the enduring legacy it leaves, and the significance of a lifelong commitment to love and faith in God.

8.2 The Journey's End and New Beginnings

As we conclude this book, it's important to acknowledge that the end of one chapter is often the beginning of another. The completion of courtship and the establishment of a godly marriage mark a new phase in the couple's life journey.

8.3 The Legacy of Love

A godly marriage is more than just a commitment between two individuals;

it's a legacy of love. This section explores how the love shared within a Christian marriage impacts not only the couple themselves but also their family, friends, and community.

8.4 Passing on Faith and Values

One of the most significant legacies of a godly marriage is the passing on of faith and values to the next generation. This chapter discusses the role of parents in raising children who understand the importance of a Christ-centered marriage.

8.5 The Continued Walk with God

Courtship in Christ is an ongoing journey of growing closer to God. As the couple's marriage matures, they must continue to seek God's guidance and deepen their faith. This section emphasizes the importance of maintaining a strong spiritual connection.

8.6 Encouraging Others

A Christian marriage can be a source of encouragement and inspiration to others. This chapter discusses how couples can serve as mentors, sharing their experiences and faith to support other couples on their own journeys.

8.7 The Role of the Church Community

The church community remains a vital part of the couple's journey even after marriage. Support, guidance, and accountability continue to be offered by the church family, helping to strengthen and sustain the marriage.

8.8 Conclusion

As we close this final chapter, we reflect on the remarkable journey of

"Courtship in Christ" and the enduring legacy it leaves. A godly marriage, founded on love, faith, and commitment to God, is a testament to the power of faith in the lives of individuals and the community. It serves as an inspiration to all those who seek to embark on their own paths toward a Christ-centered marriage, filled with love, companionship, and a deep connection with God.

9

Resources and Additional Guidance

9.1 Introduction

In this final chapter of "Courtship in Christ: A Path to Godly Marriage," we provide readers with valuable resources and additional guidance to support and enhance their journey towards a godly marriage. Here, you will find recommendations for books, organizations, and other tools that can provide further insights and assistance.

9.2 Recommended Reading

This section presents a curated list of books that address various aspects of courtship, Christian marriage, and spiritual growth. These books cover topics such as communication, conflict resolution, and deepening one's faith.

9.3 Online Resources

The internet offers a wealth of resources for individuals and couples seeking guidance in their courtship and marriage journey. This section provides links to reputable websites, blogs, and forums dedicated to Christian courtship, marriage, and family life.

9.4 Counseling and Mentorship

Counseling and mentorship are valuable tools for navigating the challenges of courtship and marriage. This section highlights the importance of seeking guidance from experienced counselors and mentors who can offer personalized support.

9.5 Church and Community Involvement

Active involvement in one's church and Christian community is a crucial aspect of courtship and marriage. This section offers guidance on finding the right church and community groups, as well as suggestions for how to engage and contribute effectively.

9.6 Marriage Enrichment Programs

Marriage enrichment programs and retreats can provide opportunities for couples to strengthen their bond and deepen their faith. This section outlines the benefits of participating in such programs and provides recommendations for reputable organizations that offer them.

9.7 Support Organizations

Support organizations exist to assist individuals and couples in their journey toward a godly marriage. This section presents information on various Christian organizations that focus on marriage support, family life, and faith-based guidance.

9.8 Conclusion

In this final chapter, we've provided a wealth of resources and additional guidance to assist readers on their path toward a godly marriage. It is our hope that these tools and recommendations will help individuals and couples as they embark on their journey of courtship in Christ, fostering a lifelong commitment to love, faith, and a strong, Christ-centered relationship.

10

A Lifelong Journey of Love, Faith, and Commitment

10.1 Introduction

In this concluding chapter of "Courtship in Christ: A Path to Godly Marriage," we reflect on the overarching themes of this journey and the enduring principles that guide a Christ-centered marriage. This chapter emphasizes that the pursuit of a godly marriage is not a destination but an ongoing, lifelong journey filled with love, faith, and unwavering commitment.

10.2 The Journey of a Lifetime

A godly marriage is a lifelong journey. It is not a destination to be reached but an ongoing, evolving relationship that requires continued nurturing, growth, and devotion. This section underscores that a Christ-centered marriage is not a mere phase but a way of life.

10.3 Love as a Daily Choice

Love in a Christian marriage is not confined to a momentary emotion but an active choice. This chapter delves into the concept that love is a daily commitment to put one's spouse's well-being and happiness above one's own, mirroring Christ's selfless love for the Church.

10.4 Faith as the Anchor

Faith serves as the anchor of a godly marriage. It is the unwavering belief in God's plan for the union and the understanding that through faith, challenges can be overcome, and blessings multiplied. This section explores the enduring role of faith in the journey of love and commitment.

10.5 The Ever-Present Role of God

Throughout the journey of courtship and marriage, God remains an ever-present source of guidance, strength, and comfort. This chapter discusses how a Christ-centered marriage continuously turns to God in prayer, gratitude, and trust.

10.6 Reflection and Gratitude

Reflecting on the journey is essential in a godly marriage. This section encourages couples to reflect on their love story, to express gratitude for each other and for God's presence in their lives.

10.7 Passing the Torch

A Christ-centered marriage leaves an enduring legacy, not only for the couple themselves but for their children, family, and community. This chapter emphasizes the responsibility of passing on the principles of love, faith, and commitment to future generations.

10.8 Conclusion

In this final chapter, we celebrate the lifelong journey of love, faith, and commitment that is "Courtship in Christ: A Path to Godly Marriage." A Christ-centered marriage is a testament to the enduring power of faith, selfless love, and unwavering commitment to God and one another. As couples continue their journey, they are encouraged to embrace the ongoing nature of a godly marriage, a journey that is deeply fulfilling, enriching, and eternally blessed.

11

Embracing Godly Marriage in a Changing World

11.1 Introduction

In this chapter of "Courtship in Christ: A Path to Godly Marriage," we address the challenges and opportunities that Christian couples face in an ever-changing world. Marriage is an institution deeply rooted in tradition, but it must adapt to the shifting dynamics of society while remaining true to its spiritual foundation.

11.2 Marriage in a Changing World

The dynamics of relationships and marriage are evolving, influenced by shifts in societal values, gender roles, and the influence of technology. This section explores the changes that modern couples experience and the implications for courtship and Christian marriage.

11.3 Navigating Technology and Social Media

Technology and social media have become integral parts of our lives. This chapter discusses how couples can harness these tools to strengthen their marriage while being mindful of their potential to cause distraction or harm.

11.4 The Role of Faith in Modern Relationships

In a rapidly changing world, faith remains a steadfast anchor in courtship and marriage. This section emphasizes the enduring role of faith in guiding Christian couples through the challenges and uncertainties of modern times.

11.5 Adapting to New Family Structures

Modern families take on diverse structures, from blended families to same-sex couples raising children. This chapter delves into how Christian values can be upheld within these changing family dynamics.

11.6 Maintaining Values in a Secular World

As Christian couples engage with secular aspects of society, they face the challenge of maintaining their values and faith. This section offers strategies for living authentically within a secular world while upholding one's Christian principles.

11.7 Embracing Diversity and Inclusivity

Embracing diversity and inclusivity is essential in today's world. This chapter discusses how Christian couples can foster an inclusive, loving environment that reflects Christ's message of love for all.

11.8 Conclusion

As we conclude this chapter and our journey through "Courtship in Christ: A Path to Godly Marriage," we recognize that embracing godly marriage in a changing world is both a challenge and an opportunity. By maintaining faith, adapting to societal changes, and upholding Christian values, couples can navigate the complexities of modern life while forging a Christ-centered marriage that is deeply meaningful, resilient, and enduring.

12

A Lifelong Covenant of Love and Faith

12.1 Introduction

In this final chapter of "Courtship in Christ: A Path to Godly Marriage," we culminate our journey by emphasizing that a Christian marriage is more than a commitment; it's a lifelong covenant filled with love and faith. It is a testament to the enduring power of love and faith in God.

12.2 A Lifelong Covenant

Christian marriage is not merely a commitment but a sacred covenant. This section explores the depth of this covenant, highlighting the difference between a covenant and a contract. It underscores the sacred, enduring nature of the marital union.

12.3 The Love that Endures

A godly marriage is marked by love that endures through all circumstances. This chapter delves into the aspects of love that stand the test of time, based on the love described in 1 Corinthians 13, which is patient, kind, not easily angered, and never fails.

12.4 The Role of Faith

Faith is the cornerstone of a Christ-centered marriage. This section emphasizes the importance of faith as the source of strength, guidance, and unity within the marriage. It highlights the significance of walking in faith together throughout life's journey.

12.5 Overcoming Challenges

Every marriage faces challenges, but a godly marriage is equipped to overcome them. This chapter discusses the power of faith and love in conquering obstacles, whether they be personal, relational, or external.

12.6 A Legacy of Love and Faith

A Christian marriage leaves a lasting legacy. This section explores the legacy of love and faith that couples create for their families, their community, and future generations. It is a testament to the power of faith and love as guiding principles.

12.7 Celebrating the Journey

In the final chapter, we celebrate the journey of "Courtship in Christ" and the enduring covenant of love and faith it represents. We reflect on the challenges and joys, the trials and triumphs, and the enduring commitment to God and each other.

12.8 Conclusion

As we conclude our exploration of "Courtship in Christ: A Path to Godly Marriage," we recognize that a Christian marriage is a lifelong covenant filled with love and faith. It is a testament to the enduring power of these principles in guiding and sustaining a deep, meaningful, and resilient marriage. Couples who embark on this journey are blessed with a commitment that enriches not only their lives but also the lives of those around them, reflecting God's divine plan for love, faith, and unity.

Book Summary: Courtship in Christ - A Path to Godly Marriage

"Courtship in Christ: A Path to Godly Marriage" is a comprehensive and insightful guide that explores the journey of courtship and marriage within the context of Christian faith. This book serves as a valuable resource for individuals and couples who seek to establish a Christ-centered marriage that is deeply rooted in love, faith, and unwavering commitment.

The book is divided into twelve chapters, each addressing specific aspects of the courtship and marriage journey within the Christian context.

Chapter 1: Courtship in Christ - A Timeless Pursuit
   - The book begins by highlighting the timeless desire for love, companionship, and lasting commitment in a rapidly changing world.
   - It introduces the concept of "Courtship in Christ," emphasizing the role of faith and spirituality in the pursuit of a godly marriage.

Chapter 2: The Biblical Foundation of Courtship in Christ
   - This chapter explores the fundamental principles of courtship as outlined in the Bible.
   - It delves into God's design for marriage, the importance of love, selflessness, and sacrifice, and the role of faith in seeking God's will.

Chapter 3: Navigating the Early Stages of Courtship in Christ
   - The book progresses to the early stages of courtship, where couples begin to establish the foundation of their relationship.
   - Topics covered include the initial connection, getting to know each

other, prayer and discernment, setting boundaries, and the role of family and community.

Chapter 4: Deepening the Connection: Courtship and Engagement
   - This chapter explores the transition from the early stages of courtship to a more committed and serious relationship, including engagement.
   - It highlights the importance of strengthening the spiritual bond, making marriage vows, and preparing for a godly marriage.

Chapter 5: The Godly Union: Christian Marriage and Beyond
   - The wedding ceremony and the marriage vows are the focus of this chapter, emphasizing the sacred nature of Christian marriage.
   - It addresses the role of the church community, maintaining purity, and preparing for the wedding.

Chapter 6: Navigating Life Together: Communication, Challenges, and Family
   - This chapter discusses the intricacies of married life, including effective communication, addressing common challenges, and the role of family and community.
   - It underscores the importance of growing together in faith and love.

Chapter 7: Growing Together in Faith and Love
   - The lifelong journey of deepening the spiritual bond and maintaining a strong connection is the focus of this chapter.
   - It encourages couples to engage in activities that foster spiritual growth, emphasize acts of service and love, and overcome challenges together.

Chapter 8: An Enduring Legacy: Reflecting on Courtship in Christ
   - The book reflects on the profound journey of courtship in Christ and the lasting legacy it leaves.
   - Topics include passing on faith and values, the continued walk with God, and the role of the church community.

Chapter 9: Resources and Additional Guidance
 - This chapter provides readers with valuable resources and recommendations for books, online resources, counseling, mentorship, and support organizations.
 - It assists couples in accessing additional guidance and support for their journey.

Chapter 10: Embracing Godly Marriage in a Changing World
 - The book acknowledges the challenges and opportunities that Christian couples face in a changing world.
 - It discusses the role of faith in modern relationships, navigating technology and social media, and embracing diversity and inclusivity.

Chapter 11: A Lifelong Covenant of Love and Faith
 - This chapter emphasizes that Christian marriage is a lifelong covenant filled with love and faith.
 - It explores the enduring aspects of love and faith that sustain a godly marriage.

Chapter 12: A Lifelong Journey of Love, Faith, and Commitment
 - In the final chapter, the book culminates with a focus on the lifelong journey of love, faith, and commitment in a Christian marriage.
 - It underscores the difference between a covenant and a contract and highlights the importance of embracing the enduring nature of marriage.

"Courtship in Christ: A Path to Godly Marriage" is a guide that not only provides practical advice but also emphasizes the spiritual and emotional aspects of courtship and marriage. It encourages readers to build a strong foundation of love, faith, and commitment, ensuring that their marriage is a lifelong covenant that reflects Christ's love for His Church.

www.ingramcontent.com/pod-product-compliance
Lightning Source LLC
LaVergne TN
LVHW010439070526
838199LV00066B/6085